The French Invasion of Italy in 1494: The History and Legacy of the Conflict that Started the Italian Wars

By Charles River Editors

Vasari's painting of the Battle of Marciano

About Charles River Editors

Charles River Editors provides superior editing and original writing services across the digital publishing industry, with the expertise to create digital content for publishers across a vast range of subject matter. In addition to providing original digital content for third party publishers, we also republish civilization's greatest literary works, bringing them to new generations of readers via ebooks.

Sign up here to receive updates about free books as we publish them, and visit Our Kindle Author Page to browse today's free promotions and our most recently published Kindle titles.

Introduction

A tapestry depicting the Battle of Pavia

The Italian Wars

In 1494, there were five sovereign regional powers in Italy: Milan, Venice, Florence, the Papal States and Naples. In 1536, only one remained: Venice. These decades of conflict precipitated great anxiety among Western thinkers, and Italians responded to the fragmentation, forevermore, of Latin Christendom, the end of self-governance for Italians, and the beginning of the early modern era in a myriad of ways. They were always heavily influenced by the lived experience of warfare between large Christian armies on the peninsula.

The diplomatic and military history of this 30 year period is a complex one that one eminent Renaissance historian, Lauro Martines, has described as "best told by a computer, so many and tangled are the treatises, negotiations and battles."[1] At the same time, the fighting went in tandem with the Renaissance and was influenced by it. Most historians credit the city-state of Florence as

---

[1] Lauro Martines, *Power and Imagination: City-States in Renaissance Italy* (Baltimore: Johns Hopkins Press, 1979), 277. The best overviews of the Italian Wars in English are Gene Brucker's 'A Horseshoe Nail': Structure and Contingency in Medieval and Renaissance Italy," in *Living on the Edge in Leonardo's Florence* (Berkeley, Los Angeles and London: University of California Press, 2005): 62-82 and Michael Mallet and Christine Shaw, *The Italian Wars, 1494-1559* (Harlow: Pearson, 2012). See also Jean-Louis Fournel and Jean-Claude Zancarini, *Les guerres d'Italie: Des batailles pour l'Europe (1494-1559)* (Paris: Gallimard, 2003), and Marco Pellegrini, *Le guerre d'Italia (1494-1530)* (Bologna: Il Mulino, 2009). The authoritative military history of the period is Piero Pieri, *Il Rinascimento e la crisi militare italiana* (Turin: Einaudi, 1952). The canonical source from the period itself is, of course, Francesco Guicciardini, *Storia d'Italia* (Turin: Einaudi, 1970), Book 1.

the place that started and developed the Italian Renaissance, a process carried out through the patronage and commission of artists during the late 12th century. If Florence is receiving its due credit, much of it belongs to the Medicis, the family dynasty of Florence that ruled at the height of the Renaissance. The dynasty held such influence that some of its family members even became Pope.

Among all of the Medicis, its most famous member ruled during the Golden Age of Florence at the apex of the Renaissance's artistic achievements. Lorenzo de Medici, commonly referred to as Lorenzo the Magnificent, was groomed both intellectually and politically to rule, and he took the reins of power at just 20 years old.

Lorenzo de Medici may have not been a king, prince or duke, but he nevertheless held significant influence over all of the noble houses of the region, from Milan and Naples to the King of France. Between 1482 and 1484, Lorenzo's influence prevented a close alliance between King Louis IX of France and the city of Venice, which was at war with Ferrara. Lorenzo's personal influence helped reduce Venice's power in the region. During the Baron's War of 1485 and 1486, while Florence sided with the pope, Lorenzo favored Ferdinando of Aragon, who had close ties with Naples, giving Lorenzo the chance to attempt to negotiate an improvement in relations between the pope and Naples. While the two had once been allied against Florence, their alliance had ended with the war. Lorenzo proposed a new agreement between the two, largely centered around financial obligations, in 1489. It was accepted in 1492, creating an enduring peace for some time. Perhaps fittingly, once Lorenzo the Magnificent died, the tenuous peace would go with him, touching off the Italian Wars.

The French Invasion of Italy in 1494: The History and Legacy of the Conflict that Started the Italian Wars chronicles the decisive campaign that forever changed the Italian peninsula at the end of the 15th century. Along with pictures of important people, places, and events, you will learn about the First Italian War like never before.

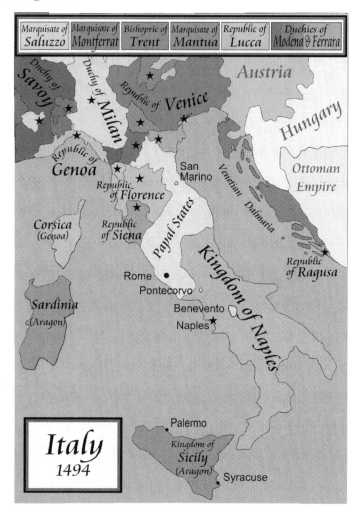

Marquisate of Saluzzo	Marquisate of Montferrat	Bishopric of Trent	Marquisate of Mantua	Republic of Lucca	Duchies of Modena & Ferrara

A map of Italy in 1494

As the head in Florence, Lorenzo de' Medici functionally served as a foreign minister throughout the 1480s, spending five to six hours a day composing letters to ambassadors, heads of state, bishops, and others. He had no formal standing, but he continued to hold power through his own ability, social network and diplomatic skills. With peace secured throughout Italy and Lorenzo's high standing both within the city, within the region and throughout Europe, both Lorenzo and the city of Florence could turn to other matters, including the arts and literature.

Lorenzo the Magnificent

The situation in Florence improved dramatically in August 1480. That month, the Ottoman Turks landed at Otranto, Italy, and since both Naples and Rome were threatened by this incursion from the east, the city-states of Italy were forced to unite against a mutual enemy. It was rumored that the Ottomans had Florentine support, but these accusations were not proven. The invasion was, nonetheless, quite favorable for Florence.

In Naples, King Ferrante returned the Tuscan possessions gained during the war and the peace treaty to Florence, while a group of ambassadors from Florence approached the pope and apologized in exchange for peace. They were absolved of sin, readmitted to the church and all sanctions were removed. The interdict on the city was also lifted, and with that Florence celebrated with bonfires and church bells. Florence had promised 15 armed galleys for the defense of Rome in return for an end to tensions with the papacy. The Ottoman Sultan died a few months later and Turkish troops left Otranto.

Though the threat ended, Lorenzo worked to maintain peace throughout Italy. His old nemesis, Girolamo Riario, continued to seek power in Romagna, and war broke out twice from 1480-1484 due to Riario, brought to an end each time through diplomatic means. The second time, the peace treaty denied Girolamo Riario several towns. Already racked by gout, Pope Sixtus IV was so upset by this that he reacted with rage, but he died in August 1484 and was succeeded by Pope Innocent VIII. Innocent VIII was far less aggressive than Sixtus IV, but he remained largely under the control of one of Sixtus' nephews, Giuliano della Rovere, early in his tenure. Riario was eventually assassinated.

Meanwhile, the city of Florence continued to control much of the surrounding area, though many of these towns, like Volterra in the early 1470s, deeply resented Florentine influence in local politics. Thus, preventing local rebellions was essential to preserve the safety and stability of the region, and Lorenzo was especially concerned about the potential for negative feelings toward Florence in the city of Pisa. Having purchased family homes both in the city and outside its walls, he invested a great deal of money in the development and improvement of Pisa, and he worked to improve relations with Pisa by expanding and developing the city's port and spending winters in Pisa with his family. The city of Pisa had long been home to Tuscany's best university, but it had fallen into disrepair, so Lorenzo funded the university, improving its standing, staff and buildings.

Marriages were one of the most valuable political tools available in Renaissance Italy, and as Lorenzo's power grew, so too did his reputation as a marriage broker. He married his own daughter Maddalena to Pope Innocent VIII's illegitimate son and brokered an advantageous marriage between his son and a relative of his wife's. These ties linked the Medici family intimately with the power structure in Rome, and as his parents did, Lorenzo broke with the tradition of marrying within the Florentine power structure. While two of his children married outside of Florence, his remaining daughters made matches with Florentine families. Lorenzo did not only arrange marriages within his own family, but among all of the prominent families of Florence. Beginning during Cosimo de' Medici's tenure in the city, the prominent families of Florence had sought Medici advice and input on their marriages.

Pope Innocent VIII

Ultimately, Lorenzo's growing relationship with the papacy enabled him to place one of his own sons, Giovanni, in a high-ranking position within the Church. Giovanni became a cardinal in the Church at his father's behest and was made a doctor of canon law at only 13. Gaining this position at such a young age was scandalous, even during the Italian Renaissance. While the news was to be kept secret until Giovanni was 16, it spread through Florence rapidly, and a later payment from the Medici bank to the pope may have been related to the revelation of the young cardinal's promotion. Giuliano's illegitimate son Giulio also entered the service of the Church. The fate of these two young cousins was intertwined throughout their lives. Giulio would gain his own cardinal's hat from Giovanni after his elevation to pope as Leo X, and Giulio would eventually become Pope Clement VII in 1523.

Pope Leo X

While the political changes in the Florentine landscape were not surprising, given the constant turbulence throughout Italy's city-states, a new religious fervor also seized the city. Friar Savonarola, a radical Dominican, had been invited into the city, first visiting in 1481 and later moving into a Dominican foundation in the city in 1489. The year before Lorenzo's death, in 1491, he gave his Lenten sermons in the cathedral of Florence, as the parish churches were too small to accommodate the crowd in attendance. Savonarola's message, while religious, was also quite democratic. His republican message, envisioning a republic for the people, sparked fear in the older, conservative elite of the city. Moreover, Savonarola preached against the excesses that he claimed were represented by the literary and artistic flourishes of the Renaissance.

Savonarola

When Lorenzo died in 1492, his son, Piero di Lorenzo de' Medici, took power in Florence. Il Magnifico had held onto power in Florence through personal magnetism and charm, but his oldest son lacked the wit, charm and intelligence of his father. He was ruthless, unforgiving and petulant, with a violent temper that often led to quarrels with his Medici cousins, Lorenzo and Giovanni di Pierfrancesco de Medici. Piero was only 22 when Lorenzo died, and though he was granted his father's role in the city upon his death, the Florentines who supported Lorenzo's position began to quietly rebel against Piero within a year of his father's death.

Piero

In the late summer of 1494, the French king, Charles VIII, crossed the Alps with a large army numbering around 30,000. He planned to take the city of Naples and had an ancestral claim to Florence's old ally, Milan.

Charles VIII

In late October 1494, Piero left Florence to meet with Charles VIII at Sarzana, a small town just outside Florence, but he did not consult with the *Otto di Pratica*, the committee in charge of foreign policy, nor did he talk to the *Signoria*, the main legislative assembly, regarding his mandate before leaving. Piero was the inheritor of a decades-long legacy of Medici control over Florentine foreign policy that had begun with his great-grandfather, Cosimo de' Medici,[2] and his clandestine diplomatic mission was in all likelihood a conscious imitation of a diplomatic victory executed by his father, Lorenzo, in 1479 during a conflict with King Ferdinand of Naples.[3] Piero, however, was not his father, and this time the circumstances were not similar. Whereas Lorenzo had been welcomed at Ferdinand of Naples' court and treated as an equal in order to defuse a tense situation in the wake of the Pazzi conspiracy and assassination of Giuliano di Pierfrancesco de' Medici, Piero arrived at Sarzana to meet with the Valois king of France who was at the head of a large and seasoned army eyeing Florentine wealth and contemplating invasion.

---

[2] Nicolai Rubinstein, *Government of Florence under the Medici*, 267.
[3] John M. Najemy, *A History of Florence, 1200-1575* (West Sussex: Blackwell, 2008), 352-361.

Lorenzo's shoes were obviously big ones to fill, and he had been respected by contemporaries as a leader whose endeavors were widely recognized as integral to peace in Italy. A Modenese diplomat had called him, in the style of grand flattery, *bilancia di senno,* the balance of sense and wisdom.[4] The term "balance of power" itself entered the political vocabulary of Western thought as a description of the tenuous peace of the late-15th century between Milan, Florence, Venice, the Papacy and Naples, and the Medici family had been central to it all.[5]

Although it would be described as a "golden age" by thinkers like Guicciardini and Machiavelli, who wrote in the wake of the political and military catastrophes of the 1520s and 1530s, the last decades of the Quattrocento were not without conflict.[6] There were, in fact, three major military and diplomatic crises over the course of 15 years that amply demonstrated the various states sought to maintain a status quo that was to their benefit. The Pazzi War (1478-1480) began in the wake of an assassination attempt on the Medici family sponsored by Pope Sixtus IV, who sought to incite a change in the Florentine government that would benefit his expansionist aims in the Romagna.[7] Full-scale violence was averted only by Lorenzo's bold voyage to Naples in 1479, when he handed himself over as hostage to Ferdinand I (Ferrante) of Naples, who eventually broke his allegiance to the Papacy.[8]

---

[4] Gino Capponi, *Storia della reppublica di Firenze* (Florence: G. Barbèra, 1876) 2:428-9.

[5] Vagt, "The Balance of Power," 95. The Treaty of Lodi has long been understood by scholars as the beginning of modern diplomacy. See Garrett Mattingly, *Renaissance Diplomacy* (London: Jonathan Cape, 1955) and Donald E. Queller, *The Office of Ambassador in the Middle Ages* (Princeton, N.J.: Princeton University Press, 1967). A more recent collection of essays has largely challenged this interpretation on a number of grounds including that it is overly focused on monarchical diplomacy, see Daniel Frigo (ed.), *Politics and Diplomacy in Early Modern Italy, the Structure of Diplomatic Practice (1450-1800)* (Cambridge: Cambridge University Press, 1999).

[6] For an overview of the political situation in Italy preceding the Italian Wars, see David Abulafia, introduction to *The French Descent into Renaissance Italy 1494-5: Antecedent and Effects* (Aldershot and Vermont: Variorum, 1995): 1-29.

[7] Lorenzo and his brother, Giuliano, were ambushed on Sunday 26 April 1478 in Santa Maria de' Fiore at the behest of Sixtus IV and the eponymous Pazzi family. Lorenzo was wounded. Giuliano was killed. See Lauro Martines, *April Blood: Florence and the Plot against the Medici* (Oxford: Oxford University Press, 2003), esp. 187-196.

[8] Legally, the kingdom of Naples was a papal fief and the popes asserted the right to confirm the ruler. Except for the conspicuous example of Clement VII's invitation to the Angevins (see below), it was not the Popes, but the rights of heredity and military prowess that determined who ruled in Naples. Good relations with the papacy, however, were essential to any claimant for two main reasons: (1) The entire northern border of the kingdom is shared with the Papal States; (2) Many of the local barons held lands in both the Papal States and the Kingdom of Naples. Both the papacy and the Neapolitan kings fermented baronial discontent to further their ends. See Christine Shaw, "The Papacy and the European Powers," in *Italy and the European Powers: The Impact of War, 1500-1530* (Leiden and Boston: Brill, 2006), 108-9.

Pope Sixtus IV

At the same time, the Turkish capture of Otranto (1480), while inspiring much outrage and many calls to arms, did not result in a collective effort on the part of any Christian powers to remove the Turks from their Apulian foothold.[9] The Ottomans withdrew from southern Italy during a succession crisis following the death of Sultan Mohammed II.

Lastly, the Neapolitan Barons' Revolt (1485), incited by Pope Innocent VIII, ended with the summary execution of the barons despite a promise of amnesty from Ferdinand. Armed conflict at an international level simmered continuously even if it never reached a rolling boil.

The precariousness of the peninsular balance of power was further exacerbated by internal discord within the governing group of individual regional powers. As Burckhardt aptly pointed out, the Italian powers were not legitimated by theories of sacral monarchy, and talent played a more important role than birth in determining who would control a city-state's government.[10] A

---

[9] Margaret Meserve offers a compelling analysis of one intellectual response to the Turkish threat: a rewriting of their origin myths in Western historical texts. See *Empire of Islam in Renaissance Historical Thought* (Cambridge, MA.: Harvard University Press, 2008).

good example of the abrogation of the laws of inheritance could be found in Milan, where Ludovico Sforza ruled instead of his nephew, Duke Giangaleazzo Sforza II (1476-1494). His search for a veneer of legitimacy inspired him to pay the enormous sum of 440,000 ducats to Maximilian Hapsburg, the Holy Roman Emperor, as a dowry for his niece, Bianca Maria Sforza.[11] The marriage took place on March 16, 1494,[12] and the ducal title was conferred on Ludovico Sforza by imperial decree on September 5 of that year.[13]

Sforza

---

[10] Jacob Burckhardt, *The Civilisation of the Renaissance in Italy*, trans. S. G. C. Middlemore (London: Allen and Unwin, 1921), 16-21.
[11] On strategies of legitimation in Sforzan Milan, see D. M. Bueno de Mesquita, "The Sforza Prince and his State," in *Florence and Italy: Renaissance Studies in Honour of Nicolai Rubinstein,* ed. Peter Denley and Caroline Elam (London: Westfield College, 1988), 161-172; D. M. Bueno de Mesquita, "Ludovico Sforza and his Vassals," *Italian Renaissance Studies* (New York: Barnes and Noble, 1960): 184-216.
[12] Joachim Whaley, *Germany and the Holy Roman Empire*, Vol. 1 (Oxford: Oxford University Press, 2011), 71.
[13] Cecilia M. Ady, *A History of Milan under the Sforza* (New York: G. P. Putnam's Sons, 1907), 148-9.

Although the Florentine government had not undergone an upheaval upon the death of Lorenzo, the acquiescence of the patrician class to rule by an inexperienced (and apparently arrogant) young man was uncertain and untested. The very institution of Papal government, with its short reigns and elective selection process, made Papal control over its lands tenuous at best, and in many cases the families of the great barons, like the Orsini and Colonna, held real power in these areas.[14]

The Venetian Republic was the only regional power not chronically weakened by factionalism and discord, so Venetian foreign policy consisted largely of upsetting the balance of power whenever it would be beneficial.[15] These political challenges to unity were combined with a strong sense of regional loyalties. Historical disunity and conflict and urban polities rife with faction were strong centrifugal forces that undermined any unifying sense in Italy. This, however, is not to say that the inhabitants of the peninsula did not conceive of themselves as a distinct group that shared in common a Roman past, the Latin language, the Catholic Church, the Italian vernaculars, and an urban environment. Rather, the forces of "division and fragmentation," as described by Gene Brucker, created a political landscape that was fragile and vulnerable to external threats as each major power privileged its own concerns over peninsular peace, the *quietà d'Italia*.[16]

The Italian regimes faced three distinct external challenges in the late-15th century. From the east, Ottoman expansionism induced fear and, sometimes, rallying calls for a new crusade. The Venetian colonies in the Adriatic were especially vulnerable, and Venice devoted efforts to defending its interests against the Turkish threat. From the west, the Aragonese-Castilian state sought to reintegrate the lands left to Ferdinand I of Naples, illegitimate son of Alfonso the Magnanimous, into their domains as a springboard for their own territorial expansion into the Mediterranean and against the Ottomans.[17] Lastly, from the north, the house of Valois, with claims to the Neapolitan throne, sought to expand its domain to include the Italian Mezzogiorno,

---

[14] Christine Shaw, "The Roman barons and the French descent into Italy," in *The French Descent into Renaissance Italy*, ed. David Abulafia (Aldershot: Variorum, 1995): 249-261.
[15] Frederick C. Lane, *Venice: A Maritime Republic* (Baltimore and London: Johns Hopkins University Press, 1973), especially 87-91; *Ibid.*, 235; Nicolai Rubinstein, "Italian Reactions to Terraferma Expansion in the Fifteenth Century," *Studies in Italian History in the Middle Ages and the Renaissance*, ed. Giovanni Ciapelli II (Rome: Edizioni di storia e della letteratura, 2004): 261-285.
[16] Gene Brucker, "From *Campanilismo* to Nationhood," *Living on the Edge in Leonardo's Florence*, 44. Vincent Illardi argues that the diplomatic correspondence of the late fifteenth-century demonstrates how foreign affairs played a substantial role in Italian political decision-making in "Towards the Tragedia d'Italia: Ferrante and Galeazzo Maria Sforza, friendly enemies and hostile allies," in *The French Descent into Renaissance Italy* (Aldershot: Variorum, 1995), 91-122.
[17] See Andrew W. Devereux, "The Other Side of Empire: the Mediterranean and the Origins of a Spanish Imperial Ideology, 1479-1516," (Ph.D diss., Johns Hopkins, 2011).

the southern portion of the peninsula which now comprises the regions of Abruzzo, Apulia, Basilicata, Campania, Calabria, Molise and Sicily.

It would be the French who first disrupted the balance of power in the late 15th century.

The French Evolution

In 1494, the French force led by Charles VIII that was encamped at Sarzana had roughly 20,000 cavalry and 15,000 infantrymen. There were also over 40 cannons, each pulled by a team of four horses, capable of launching metal rather than stone projectiles at fortress walls. The effectiveness of this artillery had been firmly established at the battles of Mordano (October 19) and Fivizzano (October 26). French military technology was not the only revolutionary aspect of this conflict, because their tactics were also radically different from anything previously seen on Italian soil. The French column was a cosmopolitan force that, along with a strong Italian component, included 8,000 Swiss soldiers whose square-formation of pikesmen had proved a surprisingly quick-footed counter to cavalry for King Louis XI against Charles the Bold of Burgundy.[18]

Furthermore, the French troops actively targeted the civilian population. At Fivizzano they took no prisoners and put men, women and children, layman and clergyman alike, to death. Charles VIII, unlike Ferdinand of Aragon some 25 years earlier, was not interested in maintaining the status quo. In fact, he sought to radically change the political landscape of Italy by making good a claim, inherited as part of his Angevin patrimony, to the throne of the kingdom of Naples. He did not intend to do so at a negotiating table, but rather with men and might. Surrender did not prevent a slaughter.

The French ability to field and control such a vast, aggressive force on foreign terrain was the result of a long process of consolidation by the French Crown that finally bore fruit in the last decades of the *Quattrocento*.

When Charles VIII ascended to the French throne in 1491, the monarchy had been strengthened by military, administrative and dynastic successes over the course of the late 15th century.[19] The Hundred Years' War and the civil wars between the Armagnacs and the Burgundians had left the French countryside devastated. Land went untilled and the peasantry migrated towards towns and other fortified places for protection. Fire, as ever, proved more of a weapon of destruction than swords or lances.[20]

---

[18] Marco Pellegrini, *Le guerre d'Italia*, 40-3.

[19] Charles VIII inherited the Crown in 1483 at the age of 13, but his sister and her husband, Anne of France and Peter II of Bourbon, ruled as regents until 1491.

[20] Robert Boutruche, "The Devastation of Rural Areas during the Hundred Years War and the Agricultural Recovery of France," in *The Recovery of France in the fifteenth century*, ed. P. S. Lewis, trans. G.F. Martin (New York: Harper Row, 1972): 23-59. Originally published as "La

However, the Hundred Years' War finally ended in 1453 to the advantage of the French, and this success was in large part due to a series of military reforms that brought control of the French knights directly under the monarchy. When Louis XI succeeded to the throne, he continued his father's attempts at controlling the powerful French barons.[21] The death of Charles the Bold at the Battle of Nancy on January 5, 1477 brought to an end the Burgundian Wars and brought peace to a population long terrorized by troops described as *écorcheurs* (flayers).[22]

Dévastation des campagnes pendant la guerre de Cent ans et la réconstruction de la France," *Mélanges 1945, III: Études historiques* (Publications de la Faculté des Lettres de Strasbourg), 127-63.

[21] Paul Ourliac, "The Concordat of 1472: An Essay on the Relations between Louis XI and Sixtus IV," in *The Recovery of France in the fifteenth-century* ed. P.S. Lewis, trans. G. F. Martin (New York: Harper Row, 1972): 102-184. Original Publication: "Le Concordat de 1472. Étude sur les rapports de Louis XI et de Sixte IV," *Revue historique de droit français et étranger*, XXI (1942), 172-223; XXII (1943), 182.

[22] They sometimes even stripped their victims of their clothes. It was one of the great successes of Charles VII and Louis XI to have reintegrated these Great Companies of soldiers into the King's army. For one example of the effects of the *écorcheurs* on communities, see René Fédou, "Une Révolte populaire à Lyon au Xve siècle. La Rebeyne de 1436," *Cahiers d'histoire publiés par les Universités de Clermont-Lyon-Grenoble*, III (1958): 129-149.

King Louis XI

King Louis XI enacted a series of fiscal reforms, including a reduction of the *taille* in the regions most affected by the famine of 1481, and encouraged economic recovery by sponsoring innovation in mining and textile production. Thanks to the principles of appanage, when Rene of Anjou died in 1480 without an heir, his holdings reverted to the Crown. A wise marriage to Anne of Brittany in 1488 expanded the borders of the French state to 450,000 km (modern metropolitan France is approx. 550,000 km). The acquisition of Marseilles, an important Mediterranean port, rekindled the hegemonic and expansionist dreams of King Louis XI and Charles of Anjou, couched now, as ever, in terms of a Christian crusade against heretics (Byzantium) and/or the infidel (Islam) for the recovery of the Holy Land.

With that, France was the largest state in Western Europe and now had a well-funded military with no wars to fight on French soil. The Italian peninsula was an obvious starting point for ambitious plans, both because of its unique geographic location at the center of the Mediterranean and its vast resources in terms of wealth and networks to far off lands. Louis XI left his son a secure, revenue-generating kingdom and subjects rather than vassals.[23] His successors followed an almost identical path, building on the fiscal and administrative reforms that made vast military projects, like an invasion of Italy, feasible.

French foreign policy had been entangled in Italy's peninsular politics ever since Charlemagne's 774 intervention in the conflict between Pope Adrian I and the Lombards. The French king maintained a web of alliances with the Italian powers.[24] Whereas Louis XI had largely ignored any obligations stemming from his agreements with the individual Italian powers, Charles VIII, who acceded to the throne a young and inexperienced man, eagerly took up the opportunity to make good his claim to the Neapolitan throne. The House of Anjou had been invited to govern the kingdom of Naples in 1265 by Pope Clement IV, who sought the expulsion of the Hohenstaufen dynasty from Italy. Charles of Anjou, Louis IX's younger brother, was crowned in St. Peter's in 1266 by five cardinals and his descendants reigned in the kingdom of Naples until the childless Queen Joanna II of Naples in 1442 adopted Alfonso V, called "the Magnanimous," of Aragon. When Ludovico Sforza, the de facto ruler of Milan, invited him to challenge Aragonese rule in southern Italy, Charles VIII saw an opportunity to demonstrate his military prowess to subsequent generations. His court greedily sought the spoils, both in glory and material wealth, likely to accrue from such a campaign.

---

[23] Boutruche, "The devastation," 41-3; Barthélemy-Amédée Pocquet du Haut-Jussé, "Une Idée politique de Louis XI: la sujétion éclipse la vassalité," *Revue historique*, 226:2 (1961): 383-98.
[24] Georges Peyronnet, "The distant origins of the Italian wars: political relations between France and Italy in the fourteenth and fifteenth centuries," in *French Descent into Renaissance Italy*, ed. David Abulafia (Aldershot: Variorum, 1995): 29-47.

Alfonso V

The French countryside no longer offered up bountiful opportunities for plunder and pillage, and the regional powers of Italy were centers of conspicuous wealth. Years of a quasi-monopoly in the Mediterranean brought the Italian merchants vast riches, and Florence was a pertinent and useful example, where out of a total population of some 35,000 inhabitants, some 10,000 men and women made ends meet by laboring in the cloth trade. Florence's economy, however, was diverse and dynamic, and the most prosperous segment of the economy was banking and international commerce, from which derived the vast fortunes of families like the Medici, Pazzi, Pitti and Rucellai. A quarter of the city's wealth (calculated in 1427 to exceed 10 million florins) was concentrated in only 100 households. Cosimo de' Medici's personal fortune, estimated at 150,000 florins, exceeded that of many European monarchs.[25] Families like the Medici and Rucellai across Italy engaged in conspicuous expenditures on public building projects and adorned their churches with art projects for which Renaissance Italy became so famous.[26]

---

[25] See Gene Brucker, "Living on the Edge in Leonardo's Florence," in *Living on the Edge in Leonardo's Florence* (Berkeley, Los Angeles and London: University of California Press, 2005), 115; Raymond de Roover, *The Rise and Decline of the Medici Bank, 1397-1494* (Cambridge, MA.: Harvard University Press, 1963), esp. 31-34. A florin contained 3.5g of gold in 1427. Today, on the gold market, 3.5g of gold is worth approx. 200 USD. Using current gold prices, Cosimo was worth 29 million USD and the city's wealth in 1497 was almost 2 billion USD.

Although posterity has not been kind to Piero de' Medici, his response to the size of the French force and their determination to extract money and safe passage from the Florentines is not surprising. Within less than a week, on November 1, 1494, he acquiesced to all of Charles VIII's demands. The French campaign in Italy was almost immediately recognized as a watershed in Italian history, and the invasion ended a centuries-long practice of self-governance by the Italian city-states. The fury and cruelty of the French forces was shocking and unthinkable to Italian onlookers, who had grown accustomed to a more diplomacy-based warfare enacted by small mercenary forces with few pitched battles. Before 1494, death tolls were counted in hundreds rather than thousands.[27]

While Piero certainly believed he acted to protect the city of Florence, the Florentines did not believe these concessions, including the city of Pisa, were necessary. Piero returned to Florence on November 8, 1494, but when he attempted to enter the palace of the Lord Priors on November 9, he was turned away and only granted permission to enter without his guard. Piero refused, and with that his family and his two younger brothers fled the city that day for Venice, by way of Bologna. They carried as much of the family's wealth with them as they were able. Before they left, Giovanni de Medici, already a cardinal, disguised himself as a Dominican friar and took a large number of books from the family's library to that at the church of San Marco.

The face of Florence had changed in a single day. Medici friends and supporters now disavowed the family and a crowd broke into homes of those closest to the Medici. The Eight tried several associates of the Medici family, including Antonio di Bernardo Dini, who had helped Lorenzo embezzle funds from the city. While Medici allies left the city, some 100 exiles were called back to Florence from exile elsewhere in Italy. Sanctions placed by Leonardo, including those against the Pazzi family, were lifted at once, and the Pazzi family was allowed to reclaim their assets in the city. Former Medici allies soon made new allegiances, voting in favor of former enemies, including the Pazzi. A new law banned marriages outside of the city to princely or noble families. A group of Florentine delegates ventured to Pisa at once, hoping to improve the terms of surrender negotiated by Piero.

Other Foreign Interests

At the time, France was not the only European monarchy making claims to the Neapolitan crown. In 1494, the House of Aragon ruled Naples and had done so since 1442. Alfonso V (the Magnanimous) of Aragon reigned over a vast conglomerate of lands including Barcelona, Malta, Valencia, Sicily and Naples.

---

[26] Leonardo da Vinci was painting his famous *Last Supper* during the 1490s for Ludovico Sforza. On artistic patronage in fifteenth-century Italy, see Dale V. Kent, *Cosimo de' Medici and the Florentine Renaissance: The Patron's Oeuvre* (New Haven and London: Yale University Press, 2000).

[27] Mallett and Shaw, *The Italian Wars*, 20-25.

Upon his death in 1458, however, two parallel familial branches were established. His illegitimate son Ferdinand I, known as Ferrante, inherited the Kingdom of Naples. Aragonese possessions in Iberia were bequeathed to Alfonso's younger brother, Giovanni II, and subsequently Giovanni's son Ferdinand of Aragon, known as the Catholic.[28] Ferrante faced some opposition to his reign, but not from his cousin's lands, where the houses of Aragon and Castile were primarily concerned with the *Reconquista* of Spain.[29] While Ferrante asserted his control in the Neapolitan kingdom by force against an attack from Anjou and the barons of the Mezzogiorno in revolt, the Catholic Monarchs, Ferdinand II of Aragon and Isabella, likewise consolidated the power of the united Castilian-Aragonese monarchy.

Ferdinand I

[28] See Alan Ryder, *Alfonso the Magnanimous, King of Aragon, Naples and Sicily, 1396-1458* (Oxford: Clarendon Press, 1990), 201-421, esp. 410-421.
[29] J. H. Elliott, *Imperial Spain, 1469-1716* (London: Penguin, 2002), esp. chapters 1-4; H. Kamen, *Spain, 1469-1714: A Society of Conflict* (New York: Longman, 1983), esp. 1-61; David Abulafia, *The Western Mediterranean Kingdoms, The Struggle for Dominion 1200-1500* (London and New York: Longman, 1997), esp. 235-245.

The Catholic Monarchs

The efforts of Isabella and Ferdinand brought great benefits to the kingdom of Naples. Jews from across the Spanish domains fled to Naples and were welcomed by Ferrante. In fact, Naples was a safe harbour for more than just religious refugees during the 15th century. The humanist and poet Giovanni Pontano founded the Accademia Pontaniana (still extant), and Italian intellectuals, among them many Florentines such as the reformed pornographer Francesco Bandini, flocked to the Neapolitan court.[30]

Southern Italy, however, was a difficult land to govern then as now, and the house of Aragon-Naples was constantly beset with challenges from the powerful barons of the Mezzogiorno. Although they successfully maintained control of the Neapolitan kingdom in the decades leading up to the French invasion, this success was in large part due to Milanese support for their rule.[31]

The breakdown in this relationship during the reign of Ferrante and under Galeazzo Maria and Ludovico il Moro was the first in a series of fatal blows to the house of Aragon-Naples. Conflict between the Sforza and Aragon-Naples, who had been allies against Papal interests for decades, circled around the figure of the duchess Isabella of Aragon, the daughter of Alfonso VI of Aragon and the wife of Giangaleazzo Sforza, from whom Ludovico had usurped power. [32] While Ferrante reigned in Naples, his granddaughter's complaints to her father, the Duke of Calabria, went unheeded, but when Alfonso came to power in 1494, Ludovico was fearful of what

---

[30] David Abulafia, *The Western Mediterranean Kingdoms*, 230-34.

[31] David Abulafia, "The inception of the reign of King Ferrante I of Naples: the events of summer 1458 in the light of documentation from Milan," in *The French Descent into Renaissance Italy 1494 -5*, edited by David Abulafia (Aldershot and Vermont: Variorum, 1995), 85-9.

[32] Ryder, *Alfonso the Magnanimous*, 411.

Neapolitan support for his nephew might bring.[33] He turned to a rival claimant to the Neapolitan throne, Charles VIII of France, for aid.

The specific invitation to cross the Alps by the de facto duke of Milan, Lodovico Sforza, was only the last in a lengthy list of such appeals. The Venetian Republic had pleaded for intervention during the Ferrara War (1484), and Pope Innocent VIII had done so twice, during the Barons' War in 1486 and again in 1489.[34]

The French Invasion

Given this background, plans for a French invasion were years in the making,[35] and the young king, heavily influenced by chivalric tales and his men of finance, had begun his preparations for conquering Naples as a base from which to launch a crusade in 1491.[36] Two key events were the catalysts for these plans. The first was the arrival of Cardinal Giuliano della Rovere at Avignon in May 1494. The holder of the see at Vincula, Giuliano della Rovere, and Rodrigo Borgia quarreled upon the latter's election to the Papal throne as Pope Alexander VI.[37] After months of intrigue and a failed assassination plot, della Rovere sailed from Ostia to France, where he joined his voice to the chorus inciting Charles VIII to war. Giuliano della Rovere's connections in his native Genoa made him a formidable ally in that he was able to help the French king raise the necessary funds for an invasion from Ligurian moneylenders.

---

[33] Ady, *A history of Milan*, 142-52.

[34] Brucker, "The Horseshoe Nail," 77-8.

[35] For details on the preparation for the expedition to Naples, see Ivan Cloulas, *Charles VIII et le mirage italien* (Paris: Albin Michel, 1986), esp. 38-56; Anne Denis, *Charles VIII et les italiens: histoire et mythe* (Geneva: Droz, 1979), esp. 10-11.

[36] Peyronnet, "Distant Origins," 48-9.

[37] Giuliano della Rovere had been a main player in church politics since the reign of Sixtus IV (his uncle). He was instrumental in the election of Innocent VIII and was a pillar of the latter's administration. Christine Shaw points out that despite frequent claims that Rodrigo Borgia and Giuliano della Rovere were already at odds before the papal election , we have no documentary evidence to support such a claim. See Christine Shaw, *Julian II: The Warrior Pope* (Oxford: Blackwell, 1993), esp. 50-96.

Pope Alexander VI

The second was the arrival of the news of the death of Ferrante on January 28, 1494. Ferrante's heir, Alfonso of Naples, was notoriously unpopular with the Neapolitan barons due to his bloody involvement in the Barons' Wars of the previous decades. The death of Ferrante left the pope with a momentous decision to make. He could choose to support the reign of Alfonso II, in light of his alliance with Spain and the Neapolitan ruling family, or he could choose to allow Charles VIII to take the city. He first attempted, diplomatically, to negotiate a peaceful solution, but when that failed he sided with Naples, a decision marked by the presence of the cardinal of Naples at the Easter Mass that year.

At the same time, the conflict divided Europe and the College of Cardinals. Giuliano della Rovere and his followers supported the French, Ascanio Sforza sided with Milan, and the Spanish cardinals supported Naples and Spain. That summer, with the blessing of the pope, Alfonso II was crowned. Jofre Borgia carried the crown.

Meanwhile, the Sforza family began to rally its troops to assist the French, and Giovanni Sforza, as Lord of Pesaro, sent information about the papal troops to Milan. Venice was officially neutral, while both Florence and the Papal States were simply unable to defend themselves against either French or Neapolitan armies.

As Charles VIII prepared to proceed south across the Alps, Neapolitan forces moved north, planning to take Milan by land and Genoa by sea. These two expeditions, in the summer of 1494, were poorly managed and failed. The French army, consisting of 25,000 men, crossed into Italy. While the infantry and cavalry, including eight thousand Swiss mercenaries, was a threat, the French artillery and cannon was much more worrisome. While Charles VIII allied with Ludovico Sforza in Milan, the Colonna family seized Ostia in the papal states for France. Florence and the surrounding area offered Charles VIII passage through their lands, surrendering without a fight.

Pope Alexander VI nevertheless invested Alfonso of Naples as the head of the house of Aragon-Naples. Thus, the French invasion of Italy also doubled as an effort at ecclesiastical reform brought about by the Most Christian King of France, Charles VIII, and a strong, combative member of the upper echelon of a church corrupted by a simoniacal pope.[38] On March 13, 1494, Charles VIII took the title of King of Jerusalem and Sicily at Lyon. After a summer of foot-dragging that lulled Alfonso of Naples into a false sense of security for the upcoming winter, French troops crossed from France into Italy on September 3, 1494. Charles VIII himself sailed to Asti with the siege engines.

The King of France arrived in Asti on September 9, 1494. He was forced to remain there until October 6 because of Aragonese troops and ships that had been sent out to obstruct his itinerary by attacking Genoa and preventing the city from providing Charles VIII with a safe harbor. A combined set of Milanese and French forces, led by Louis d'Orléans, Charles VIII's cousin and the future Louis XII, pushed back the 5,000 Aragonese troops. The cannons on board the French ships were instrumental in a French naval victory at Rapallo.

Naturally, the French invasion of Italy in 1494 was shocking to Italian observers both in terms of scale and ferocity. Francesco Guicciardini was not even a teenager when the French troops crossed the Alps, and his account of Charles VIII's appearance is both vivid and emblematic of what the Italians thought. His description heavily influenced other accounts of these events, is supported by current scholarship, and his vocabulary and organization of content borrows directly from Bernardo Rucellai.[39] Guicciardini noted, "The French developed many infantry pieces which were even more manueverable [than those introduced by the Venetians at the battle of Chioggia], constructed only of bronze. These were called cannons and they used iron cannonballs instead of stone as before, and this new shot was incomparably larger and heavier than that which had been previously employed. Furthermore, they were hauled on carriages drawn not by oxen as was the custom in Italy, but by horses, with such agility of manpower and tools assigned for this purpose that they almost always marched right along with the armies and were led right up to the walls and set into position there with incredible speed; and so little time

---

[38] Michael Mallett, "Personalities and Pressures: Italian involvement in the French invasion of 1494," in *The French Descent into Renaissance Italy*, ed. David Abulafia (Aldershot: Variorum, 1995), 160.
[39] See chapters 4 & 5.

elapsed between one shot and another and the shots were so frequent and so violent was their battering that in a few hours they could accomplish what previously in Italy used to require many days. They used this diabolical rather than human weapon not only in besieging cities but also in the field."[40]

Guicciardini preceded his account of the French forces with a discussion of millenarianism and other prophetic movements present in Italy on the eve of the French invasion. Contemporary scholarship continues to place the French invasion as a watershed in Italian history, and the religious fervour of the era is a relevant context for interpreting the Italian responses to these decades of warfare on the peninsula as waged by the other European powers.[41] Guicciardini further draws readers' attention to the new tactics and technology employed by the French in the 1494 campaign.[42] He wrote, "This artillery made Charles' army all the more formidable throughout Italy; formidable, besides, not so much because of the number as for the valor of his troops. For, his men-at-arms were almost all the King's subjects and not plebeians but gentlemen whom the captains could not enlist or dismiss simply at their will; nor were they paid by the officers, but by the royal ministers. Furthermore, their companies were at full muster, the men in prime condition, their horses and arms in good order, since they were not constrained by poverty in providing for themselves."[43]

The French forces were better-equipped, and their loyalty was to the king rather than a *condottiere*. Of course, that did not stop them from wreaking havoc in the Italian countryside by raping and pillaging. Indeed, they were actively encouraged to engage in these violent activities as a conscious tactic on the part of the French military commanders. The first example of this "barbaric" behaviour was on October 19, 1494 at Mordano, where all the inhabitants of the small Romagnol town were put to death, including women and children.[44] The Italian accounts of the events, including those offered by Guicciardini and Rucellai, emphasized that the entire population, not just able-bodied men, were massacred.[45] Current scholarship explains this breaking away from a tradition of clemency to the vanquished upon their surrender as a

---

[40] Francesco Guicciardini, *A History of Italy*, trans. Sidney Alexander (New York: Macmillan, 1969), 1, XI.

[41] See Norman Cohn, *The pursuit of the millenium: revolutionary millenarians and mystical anarchists of the Middle Ages* (Oxford and New York: Oxford University Press, 1970). Cohn's thesis is that millenarianism emerges in the context of societal disaster among the marginalised of a society. The Savonarolan movement, however, poses an interesting challenge to his argument for it was publicly supported by many of Florence's leading men; see also J. R. Hale, "War and Public Opinion in Renaissance Italy," *Italian Renaissance Studies: A tribute to the late Cecilia M. Ady*, ed. E. F. Jacob (New York: Barnes and Noble, 1960): 94-122.

[42] Simon Pepper, "The Face of the Siege: Fortification, Tactics and Strategy in the early Italian Wars," in *Italy and the European powers; the impact of war, 1500-1530*, ed. Christine Shaw (Leiden and Boston: Brill, 2006): 33-56.

[43] Guicciardini, *A History of Italy*, 1, XI.

[44] I adopt, here, the terminology of the Italian observers.

[45] On Rucellai, see chapter 5. For Francesco Guicciardini, see for example the description of the sack of Fivizzano in *Storia d'Italia* (Turin: Einaudi, 1970), I, 14.

calculated attempt to strike terror in the population.[46] The fear of extermination became a powerful tool in the French arsenal.

While the events at Mordano shocked Italian observers, the siege of Sarzana only three days later reinforced the growing terror in the face of the *furia franzese*. On October 22, 1494, the French artillery bombarded the citadel of Sarzanello and demonstrated the ineffectiveness of traditional fortifications against bronze cannons that launched metal rather than stone projectiles.[47] The greater density and durability of metal projectiles was, in the end, what made 1494 the turning point in military technology rather than the invention of artillery itself. Stones weighed upwards of 300 pounds and broke upon impact, but a 50 pound metal ball caused equivalent damage and used less gunpowder. Each Italian city would have had about three or four of these cannons, whereas Charles VIII mobilized over 40 cannons each being pulled by at most two pairs of horses.[48]

Despite his advantage, Sarzana was the first and last of the great artillery bombardments by French forces during the reign of Charles VIII. Unsure of their chances against Florence itself, a much larger target capable of raising the money for mercenary troops and a city of 35,000 inhabitants who might be expected to defend their city in the tight corners of an urban setting, the French forces again chose to use scare tactics against the Florentines. Thus, they chose to attack Fivizzano not only because of its strategic location in Lunigiana, but also because it was an easy target and they were supported by the local princeling, Gabriele Malaspina, who had recently lost control of the area to the Florentines. The cruelty of the siege was unprecedented and, again, all the inhabitants who surrendered were slaughtered.[49]

The massacres at Mordano and Fivizanno yielded results. The Florentines were terrified, but divided as to the correct response to the approaching French forces. A group whose financial interests were embroiled in Naples and the Papal States did not want to turn their backs on their allies. Another group, with assets in Lyon estimated at 300,000 ducats, sought reconciliation with the French at all costs.[50] Thus, it was without the support of the Florentine governing body, the *Signoria*, that Piero de' Medici travelled to Sarzana to meet with Charles VIII in person. It was also at this juncture, in the face of the *furia franzese* and fears that the French troops would

---

[46] Pellegrini, *Le guerre d'Italia*, 29.

[47] In response to this advent in siege technology, fortifications came to be build *à la trace italienne*. See Bert S. Hall, *Weapons and Warfare in Renaissance Europe: Gunpowder, Technology, and Tactics* (Baltimore and London: Johns Hopkins Press, 1997), esp. 158-164. See also Michael Mallett, "The transformation of war, 1494-1530," in *Italy and the European Powers: The Impact of War, 1500-1530*, ed. Christine Shaw (Leiden and Boston: Brill, 2006): 3-21; Geoffrey Parker, *The Military Revolution: Military Innovation and the Rise of the West, 1500-1800* (Cambridge: Cambridge University Press, 1996).

[48] Pellegrini, *Le guerre d'Italia*, 30-32.

[49] *Ibid.*, 34.

[50] Brown, "The Revolution of 1494," 20.

winter in Milanese territory, that Ludovico Sforza offered to mediate between the two powers. Faced with the force and ferocity of French military engagement, Piero de' Medici agreed to all of Charles VIII's terms on November 1, 1494 by giving over the fortresses of Sarzana, Sarzanello, Pietrasanta, Pisa, Ripafratta and Livorno to the French king. Most likely he sought to get the French forces beyond Florentine lands as swiftly as possible. His relinquishing of Florentine-governed Pisa to French control particularly infuriated the Florentines and would remain a divisive issue for the city both in terms of domestic governance and foreign policy in the decades to come.[51]

The *Signoria* responded to Piero de' Medici's perceived treachery on November 9, 1494 by expelling him from the city and its domains *in absentia* and confiscating Medici property. Decades of Medici rule in Florence were brought to an end. Charles VIII, however, was eager to enforce the agreement and marched his army to Pisa, where he began planning the siege of Florence in order to reinstate a Medici government that would support his campaign against Naples.

Into the power vacuum in Florence stepped the Dominican friar Girolamo Savonarola, with a message of reform. From his pulpit, Savonarola argued that the scourge of the French forces was divinely inspired in order to bring about both moral and political reform. He called Charles VIII a New Cyrus and foretold of a new era of virtuous living with a reformed Florence as a "New Jerusalem." The violence was interpreted as a purgative that would cure the peninsula of its political-social illnesses.[52] His message was supported by influential political figures like Francesco Valori, and much of the general population.[53]

Florentine representatives, including Bernardo Rucellai, were dispatched to Pisa to negotiate with Charles VIII. There were three rounds of negotiations, the discussion of which took up about 10% of Rucellai's *De bello italico*. Charles VIII was convinced to spare Florence by the argument that an urban landscape was a difficult battleground for his troops. Thus, if Piero de' Medici indeed acquiesced to Charles VIII's demands in order to get the French troops out of Florentine territories as quickly as possible, his gambit was successful, because Charles VIII led his troops into Lazio before December began.[54] The Florentine government had defended the city from rape, pillage and massacre, but once the immediate crisis had been averted, factionalism continued to plague the functioning of government. A complete restructuring of the governing

---

[51] Pellegrini, *Le Guerre d'Italia*, 34-7.

[52] Jean-Louis Fournel and Jean-Claude Zancarini, *La politique de l'expérience: Savonarole, Guicciardini et le républicanisme florentin* (Turin: Edizioni dell'Orso, 2002), esp. 55-73.

[53] Donald Weinstein, *Savonarola and Florence: Prophecy and Patriotism in the Renaissance* (Princeton: Princeton University Press, 1970), esp. 112-137. See also Lauro Martines, *Fire in the City: Savonarola and the Struggle for the Soul of Renaissance Florence* (Oxford: Oxford University Press, 2006); Lorenzo Polizzotto, *The Elect Nation: The Savonarolan Movement in Florence, 1494-1545* (Oxford: Clarendon, 1994).

[54] Pellegrini, *Le guerre d'Italia,* 38.

bodies, including the introduction of a 4,000 person great council modeled on the Venetian government, was brought about in 1494, to the consternation of many of the traditional ruling families of Florence who had supported the Medici regime throughout the fifteenth century.[55]

Francesco Granacci's painting of French troopers entering Florence on November 17

As the French forces advanced towards Rome, those cardinals opposed to Alexander VI, such as Giuliano della Rovere (the future Pope Julius II) and the French Cardinal Peraud, were encouraged by Charles VIII's support of ecclesiastical reform and called for a new conclave. The army left the Tuscan town of Siena on December 4 and arrived at Montalcino, a Tuscan town under papal rule, the next day. Facing no opposition at the fortress of Acquapendente, Charles VIII rested his troops that Sunday. The king entered the city of Viterbo, about 80 kilometers north of Rome on the Via Cassia, on December 10.

---

[55] The internal Florentine political struggle is a main topic of chapter 4. On the consitutional reform in Florence, see Nicolai Rubinstein, "Politics and Constitution in Florence at the End of the Fifteenth Century," in *Italian Renaissance Studies,* ed. E. F. Jacob (London: Faber and Faber, 1960): 148-183; Butters, *Governors and Government,* 22-36.

It was clear that if a resistance was not mounted before Charles VIII crossed the natural boundaries created by Civitavecchia, Viterbo, Orvieto and Perugia, a defense of Rome would be all but impossible.[56] Ostia, the Roman port and a strong citadel, had fallen out of the control of the Roman curia and into the hands of the Colonna family (French allies since June) months earlier. The papacy was in many ways undone by the notorious perfidy of the Roman barons.[57] Upon hearing the news that Charles VIII was again on the move on December 14, Virginio Orsini, *condottiere* and head of the great baronial family, offered his castles up to king in the hopes that they would stay out of the hands of his rivals, the Colonna.[58] This left Pope Alexander VI without a military commander to oversee the defense of Rome.

Civitavecchia came under French control on December 17, and three days later the troops regrouped at Ostia. Supply lines to the city, where a small Neapolitan force under the command of Ferrandino, Duke of Calabria remained encamped, were cut. The situation was so perilous that on December 18, Pope Alexander VI and many of his cardinals sent their valuables to Naples by ship.

Even at this juncture, however, Alexander VI could not give up Rome without effectively, if not legally, abdicating. Thus, he aimed to take shelter in the Castel Sant'Angelo and withstand a protracted siege. A violent rainstorm on December 23, interpreted by many as the divine hand at play, caused a portion of the fortress walls to cave in, and Charles VIII was spared having to decide whether or not he would commit such an impiety as launching artillery at some of the holiest of Christian sites. On Christmas Day of 1494, the French king sent his terms to the pontiff: his investiture as king of Naples, custody of the Ottoman prince and brother of Bayazet, Djem (who had fled to Rome upon his brother's accession), and control of the Castel Sant'Angelo itself. In an act of clemency, either to save the Eternal City from destruction or to spare the lives of his troops, he also offered a one-day truce to Ferrandino and the Neapolitan forces that would permit them to retreat. They left Rome before daybreak by the San Lorenzo gate, and the vanguard of the French forces entered the city on December 29. The king himself arrived on New Year's Eve.[59]

---

[56] Rome itself offers little in the way of natural defences. The only other defensible boundary in the area is south of Rome and about 80 kilometres west of Naples at Montecassino where the Allied forces, predominantly Polish, fought for months before ousting the German troops from the monastery in 1945.

[57] Many of the Roman barons also held land in the kingdom of Naples and, as such, had an equal claim of loyalty to the King of Naples. See Shaw, "The Papacy," 109.

[58] Virginio Orsini was in the pay of Alfonso II of Naples. While he gave up his lands to the French, he himself went to Naples to serve the king. Charles VIII captured Virginio and Niccolò Orsini when he took Naples and Virginio lost two counties, namely Tagliacozzo and Albi. Niccolò escaped after Fornovo and Virginio was released when Charles VIII returned to Asti. See Christine Shaw, *The Political role of the Orsini family from Sixtus IV to Clement VII* (Rome: Istituto storico italiano per il Medio Evo, 2007), 180-181.

[59] Yvonne Labande-Mailfert, *Charles VIII et son milieu: 1470-1498: La jeunesse au pouvoir*

Despite his declared intention of enacting church reform and the protests of the cardinals della Rovere, Sforza, Péraud, Savelli, Lunati and others, Charles VIII did not tarry in Rome for a conclave.[60] Instead, he kept up the rapid pace of the advancement that was now four months old. On January 11, 1495, Alexander VI granted the French king and his troops safe passage to Naples, and his son, Cesare Borgia, was taken in surety for four months to ensure that the agreement was fulfilled. Alexander VI reigned another nine years.

Cesare Borgia

The French advance brought an already tense situation in the Mezzogiorno to a boiling point. Aragonese control of the countryside had been tenuous at best in the years leading up to 1494. There had been two baronial revolts, incited by the Papacy, since the peace of Lodi in 1454. The kings of Naples had harshly put down these insurrections again and again, and their brutality fostered resentment. To make matters even worse, the Neapolitans were numerically outmatched

---

(Paris: Klinckseik, 1975), 300-315.
[60] The primary source for Charles' brief stay in Rome is the journal of Johann Burchard, Alexander' VI's master of ceremonies. Johann Burchard, *At the court of the Borgia*, trans. Geoffrey Parker (London: The Folio Society, 1963), 90-120.

by the French, with 20,000 cavalry and 15,000 infantry against 5,000 or 6,000 cavalry and 12,000 footsoldiers.

The population welcomed Charles VIII as a liberator and on January 21, 1485 Alfonso II abdicated in favor of his son, Ferrandino (Ferdinand II of Naples) who, he hoped, would be better able to negotiate with the army at his doorstep.[61] Alfonso fled to Sicily and died in a monastery before the end of 1495. His abdication was trumpeted as yet another sign of divine favor for Charles VIII.

The very few strongholds of pro-Aragonese loyalty were subjected to ferocious attacks by the French troops that, in the end, would greatly undermine popular support for French rule in the Mezzogiorno. For example, at Ciociara, a small group of Aragonese barons and their community remained a thorn in Charles VIII's side by blocking his advancement to the river Liri. Rather than fighting a pitched battle at each stronghold still loyal to Ferrandino, the French forces yet again used violence against the local population to discourage any who might dare to hold out against them. The target of this exemplary savagery was Monte San Giovanni, the fief of d'Avalos, who was a naval commander for Ferrandino. The citadel was well-situated and defended by the local population rather than a mercenary force. In order to inflict a terrible punishment on these most loyal of Aragonese subjects, the French cannons were transported within reach of the town walls and pounded them for four hours; they opened three breaches in three separate places, through which three columns passed. The garrison was quickly overwhelmed and San Giovanni came under French control.

The clemency Charles VIII demonstrated at Rome was not forthcoming. Instead, in a savage reenactment of the events at Fivizzano, the defenders not killed in battle were massacred by the French forces. The vast majority of the garrison came from the local countryside, and over 700 people were put to death.[62]

Ferrandino, now King of Naples after his father's abdication earlier that month, brought his remaining troops, consisting of 4,000 cavalry and 6,000 infantry, to Capua in order to block the French advance on Naples. The *furia franzese* had, once again, taken its toll on the local population. The Capuans entreated Ferrandino to return to Naples for more reinforcements. As soon as he left the area, the city-dwellers revolted and ejected the Aragonese forces from their walls to open their arms in welcome to the French. By February 18, 1495, Charles VIII was in Capua and Naples was rioting not only against the Aragonese monarchy, but also against the administrative class that had helped it to govern. Ferrandino retreated to the island of Ischia to wait for help from his second cousin, King Ferdinand of Spain.

---

[61] On Ferrandino see Benedetto Croce, *Storie e Leggende Napoletane* (Milan: Adelphi Edizioni, 1990), 157-179.
[62] Pellegrini, *Le guerre d'Italia*, 47.

Charles VIII finally entered Naples in ceremonial garb on February 22, 1495 and was welcomed by the population as a Messiah.[63] The French invasion had taken just under six months, and Alexander VI allegedly declared that the French had won Italy "with a piece of chalk," a reference to how the French army marked the houses that would quarter their soldiers with white chalk.[64] Indeed, they had not fought a single pitched battle.

A contemporary depiction of the French entering Naples

The French Withdrawal

Venice, up until this point, had not involved itself in the power struggle on the peninsula. Venetian lands had not been in the path of the advancing French forces, and the Turkish threat to Venice's Adriatic possessions, like Cyprus and Dalmatia, were of greater concern to a maritime empire that required vast forests to maintain its fleet and grain to feed its populations.[65] A generation earlier, the Venetians had fought the Ottomans in several battles on the coastlines and

---

[63] Labande-Mailfert, *Charles VIII*, 340.

[64] Philippe de Commynes, *Mémoires* (Geneva: Droz, 2007) VII, 14: "Et, comme a dit ce pape Alexandre qui regne, les Françoys y sont alléz avecques des esperons de boys, et de la craye en la main des fourriers pour marcher logis, sans aultre peyne."

[65] Elisabeth Crouzet-Pavan, *Venice Triumphant: The Horizons of a Myth* (Baltimore: Johns Hopkins University Press, 2002), esp. 97-137; Karl Appuhn, *A Forest on the Sea: Environmental Expertise in Renaissance Venice* (Baltimore: Johns Hopkins University Press, 2009), esp. 94-143.

islands in the Aegean Sea. Venice had dominated the Mediterranean for centuries, and their fleet was superior to all other naval powers at the time, but during the series of campaigns which became known as the Ottoman-Venetian War, the scales tilted in favor of the Turks. While conquering the island of Lesbos, they also annexed Albania and Negroponte. The war ended with the Treaty of Constantinople in 1479, when the Republic of Venice agreed to cede a few important enclaves on the Dalmatian Coast to the Ottomans in exchange for peace in the ones they were allowed to keep. The treaty also imposed an annual tribute for letting Venice continue to conduct trade in the Black Sea, consequently diminishing their position as a naval trade state in the Levant.

Moreover, unlike the other Italian powers, Venice was not plagued by factions (or so they convinced themselves and others), so they did not need to rely on the help of allies to defend herself.[66] Rule by a small, tightly-knit oligarchy had brought many advantages to Venice, and unlike Hungary or Milan, it was able to withstand the death of a ruler. Furthermore, the commercial interests of this oligarchy contributed to centuries of consistent foreign policy: prevent any other power from arming a rival fleet in the Adriatic. Venetian interests on the peninsula consisted largely in disturbing the balance of power in order to benefit from the ensuing disorder by acquiring lands.[67] However, just as it was imperative that the Adriatic be free of rival powers, so too was it imperative that the peninsula be free of any power capable of challenging Venice on its own. The overwhelming success of the French advance, which brought the lion's share of the peninsula under the sway of a power capable of amassing both a large army and a substantial fleet, posed a serious threat to Venetian foreign policy.

Thus, when King Ferrandino realized that he did not have the resources on his own to regain control of the Kingdom of Naples from Charles VIII and the French army, he turned to the Venetians for aid. In return for a loan of 200,000 ducats (approximately $40 million USD today), he offered Venice the ports of Trani, Brindisi, and Otranto until the money was repaid. Apulia had always been Venice's chief source of grain and remained so even after its 15th century expansion in northern Italy. Venice had regularly intervened in the upheavals in Apulia, seeking concessions from the various rulers, combating piracy in the Adriatic and defending Christian interests against the Saracens and Turks. With this agreement, the Venetians acquired, legitimately, what they had craved for half a millennium, but they were also now committed to expelling the French from the peninsula.[68]

---

[66] Humfrey C. Butters, "Politics and Diplomacy in Late Quattrocento Italy: the Case of the Barons' War (1485-86)," in *Florence and Italy: Renaissance Studies in Honour of Nicolai Rubinstein*, ed. Peter Denley and Caroline Elam (London: Westfield College, 1988), 16. The Venetian elective body and oligarchical rule was the paradigm for harmonious urban government adopted by writers like Rucellai and Machiavelli as well as by preachers like Savonarola.
[67] See Lane, *Venice*, 201-241.
[68] Carol Kidwell, "Venice, the French invasion and the Apulian ports," in *The French Descent into Renaissance Italy*, ed. David Abulafia (Aldershot: Variorum, 1995), 298-300.

Alexander VI joined the Venetian coalition, renamed the *Lega santa* (Holy League), in early 1495. He feared that Charles VIII's promised ecclesiastical reform would actually take place now that the Neapolitan Kingdom had been brought under French control. Furthermore, the three Italian powers - Milan, Venice, and the Papacy - were joined by England and Spain, traditional rivals of the French who hoped to see the French defeated in Italy. Florence, however, remained committed to a French alliance, for it was believed that Charles VIII, having accomplished his goals on the peninsula with Florentine support, would return Pisa to Florentine subjugation.[69]

The Holy League officially aimed to combat transalpine control of the peninsula and organize an attack against the infidels. This latter goal was shared not only with Charles VIII, whose initial attempts at engaging the Turks in Albania were cut short by the challenges posed by the newly-unified Italian front, but also Renaissance humanists whose crusade literature contributed to the development of a new sense of European identity and of Eastern otherness.[70]

Without delay, the Venetians put 20,000 men into the field under the command of Francesco II Gonzaga, Marquess of Mantua. Now, Italy threatened to become a "serpents' den" for Charles VIII, as communication with the supply lines wavered, native populations became disenchanted with their "liberators," and barons reconsidered their allegiances.[71] Charles VIII decided to withdraw in late spring of 1495 and left behind 10,000 combatants and 60 artillery guns, including 16 large cannons, to defend the Kingdom of Naples against the foreseeable response from the Spanish-Aragonese line.[72]

---

[69] Nicolai Rubinstein, "The Empire," 144-5.

[70] Pellegini, *Le guerre d'Italia*, 52-3. See also Nancy Bisaha, *Creating East and West: Renaissance Humanists and the Ottoman Turks* (Philadelphia: University of Pennsylvania Press, 2004); James Hankins, "Renaissance Crusaders: Humanist Crusade Literature in the Age of Mehmed II," *Dumbarton Oaks Papers* 49 (1995): 111-207.

[71] This metaphor indeed is employed by Bernardo Rucellai to describe Italy after the battle of Fornovo. See below, pg. ???.

[72] Pellegrini, *Le guerre d'Italia*, 54-5.

Francesco II Gonzaga

Having split his forces, the numerical superiority that had been so essential to French success in 1494 was overturned. Charles lost troops to desertion and illness (especially syphilis), and he had cut his army in half to defend Naples. Gonzaga, commander of the Venetian forces, had 23,000 men, more than double the size of the French force engaged at Fornovo. The notoriety of the "indestructible" French forces still played a role in the outcome of the battle in that Gonzaga chose his terrain for engaging with French troops to counteract the strength of a French cavalry charge. This decision left the town of Pontremoli undefended against sacking by the French.

Gonzaga divided his force into three and left the Albanian contingent of his army to face the French head-on. However, when the opportunity to plunder a baggage train enriched with Neapolitan spoils presented itself, they broke formation and left the way open for a French retreat through the *val Padana*, which Ludovico Sforza had been assigned to defend. In essence, the disunity that plagued the Italian states as a whole played out on the battlefield.[73]

Charles VIII maintained control over the *Mezzogiorno* for only 16 months. The young French king had inherited his domain from a great consolidator of monarchical power, Louis XI, and was inexperienced in the art of appeasing contending factions. His troops were hated for their brutality, and his rule failed to bring about the dividends in terms of land grants and administrative positions that the barons of the *Mezzogiorno*, who had supported him in favor of the Aragonese dynasty, had anticipated. In early spring 1495, Ferrandino disembarked in Calabria and was welcomed by a populace now disenchanted with the one-time liberators who proved to be arrogant and greedy. The French forces fled to the Adriatic coast, and Venice, in exchange for the control of certain Apulian ports, namely Trani, Monopoli, Mola, Polignano,

---

[73] *Ibid.*, 57-8.

Gallipoli, Otranto and Brindisi, provided the French with help. Ferrandino and his uncle, Federico, sparked insurrections, while King Ferdinand the Catholic of Spain prepared an army in Sicily to aid his Aragonese cousins. In exchange for help from the Spanish-Aragon line, Ferrandino married his 17 year old aunt.[74]

Although primarily occupied with his holdings in Iberia, Ferdinand the Catholic had not been entirely unconcerned with his cousin's lands in southern Italy. He had sent aid during the second baronial rebellion of 1485-1486, and he had sent aid to Naples in 1495. The Spanish infantry, under the command of Gonzalo de Còrdoba, engaged with the French forces on June 28, 1495 at the First Battle of Seminara and were defeated by Charles VIII's Swiss pikesmen.[75] Nonetheless, the Aragonese forces slowly took back the Mezzogiorno and reformed their military tactics. They increased the light cavalry component in their army to better collaborate with infantry as well as enact their traditional roles of scouting, foraging and harassing a retreating enemy.[76]

Ferrandino reentered Naples to great rejoicing on July 7, 1495, but it took another year to oust the remaining French forces from their fortified positions in the city. French capitulation finally occurred on June 23, 1496, but Ferrandino was not able to enjoy the fruits of his efforts, for he fell ill three months after the expulsion of the French forces. The popular young king died in Naples on September 7, 1496.[77] He left no direct heirs.

The French and Spanish monarchies were both eager to enter into the power vacuum in the kingdom of Naples after Ferdinand II's death, but the barons and the towns backed Federigo, son of Ferrante of Naples and uncle of Ferrandino.[78] Dissatisfied, the French and Spanish monarchies rapidly sought to undermine Federico's rule in the Mezzogiorno, and their machinations culminated in the secret Treaty of Granada of 1500.[79]

---

[74] *Ibid.*, 59-60.
[75] *El Gran Capitàn*, as he was known, acquired a reputation as a protector of the Jews in Aragonese lands. See David Abulafia, "Ferdinand the Catholic and the Kingdom of Naples," in *Italy and the European Powers: The Impact of War, 1500-1530*, ed. Christine Shaw (Leiden and Boston: Brill, 2006), 153-4; Mallett, "The Transformation," 7.
[76] Mallet, "The Transformation," 11.
[77] Jerry H. Bentley, *Politics and Culture in Renaissance Naples* (Princeton, NJ.: Princeton University Press, 1987), 37.
[78] Pellegrini, *Le guerre d'Italia*, 59-61.
[79] Abulafia, "Ferdinand the Catholic," 141; Mallet and Shaw, *The Italian Wars*, 58.

I. Sailko's picture of a coin depicting Federigo

The Venetian involvement in the Holy League and the successful restoration of the Aragonese dynasty in Naples served as catalysts for the development of a political and ideological orientation that was shared by the ruling classes across the Italian peninsula. The catch phrases for this movement were *buoni italiani* and *libertà d'Italia*. These terms described the proponents of a strategic line that attempted to revive the political systems in force in Italy at a perceived time of "political balance" between the Peace of Lodi in 1454 and the French invasion of 1494.[80] As a political program, the *libertà d'Italia* demanded the expulsion of the transalpine foreigners from Italy and the reconstruction of a multi-state structure that was balanced and ruled by natives.[81] Transalpine became a synonym for foreign, and it was not immediately clear after the successes at the Battle of Fornovo and in the Mezzogiorno that these aspirations to expel the foreigners from the peninsula would ever be fully realized. Thus, the speed and magnitude of the French withdrawal was as shocking to the Italian onlookers as the previous violence brought to bear on the local populations. At the same time, the vulnerability of the Italian states, whose leaders had been powerless to stop the killing and pillaging during the French invasion, had been

---

[80] Riccardo Fubini, "Lega italica e 'politica dell'equilibrio' all'avvento di Lorenzo de' Medici al potere," in *Italia Quattrocentesca: Politica e diplomazia nell'età di Lorenzo il Magnifico* (Milan: FrancoAngeli, 1994): 185-219.

[81] Pellegrini, *Le guerre d'Italia*, 59-60.

demonstrated.

Conflict would begin anew upon King Louis XII's rise to the French throne in 1498, and Italy would serve as a theater of war for the Hapsburg and Valois monarchies until the mid-16th century, until the Peace of Cateau-Cambrésis in 1559.

Online Resources

Other books about Italy by Charles River Editors

Other books about the Italian Wars on Amazon

Further Reading

Arfaioli, Maurizio. The Black Bands of Giovanni: Infantry and Diplomacy During the Italian Wars (1526–1528). Pisa: Pisa University Press, Edizioni Plus, 2005. ISBN 88-8492-231-3.

Arnold, Thomas F. The Renaissance at War. Smithsonian History of Warfare, edited by John Keegan. New York: Smithsonian Books / Collins, 2006. ISBN 0-06-089195-5.

Baumgartner, Frederic J. Louis XII. New York: St. Martin's Press, 1994. ISBN 0-312-12072-9.

Black, Jeremy. "Dynasty Forged by Fire." MHQ: The Quarterly Journal of Military History 18, no. 3 (Spring 2006): 34–43. ISSN 1040-5992.

———. European Warfare, 1494–1660. Warfare and History, edited by Jeremy Black. London: Routledge, 2002. ISBN 0-415-27532-6.

Blockmans, Wim. Emperor Charles V, 1500–1558. Translated by Isola van den Hoven-Vardon. New York: Oxford University Press, 2002. ISBN 0-340-73110-9.

Fraser, Antonia, Mary Queen of Scots (New York: Delacorte Press, 1969).

Guérard, Albert, France: A Modern History (Ann Arbor: University of Michigan Press, 1959). ISBN 978-0-582-05758-6.

Guicciardini, Francesco. The History of Italy. Translated by Austin Parke Goddard. London: John Towers. 1753.

Guicciardini, Francesco. The History of Italy. Translated by Sydney Alexander. Princeton: Princeton University Press, 1984. ISBN 0-691-00800-0.

Hall, Bert S. Weapons and Warfare in Renaissance Europe: Gunpowder, Technology, and Tactics. Baltimore: Johns Hopkins University Press, 1997. ISBN 0-8018-5531-4.

Knecht, Robert J. Renaissance Warrior and Patron: The Reign of Francis I. Cambridge: Cambridge University Press, 1994. ISBN 0-521-57885-X.

Konstam, Angus. Pavia 1525: The Climax of the Italian Wars. Oxford: Osprey Publishing, 1996. ISBN 1-85532-504-7.

Lesaffer, Randall. Peace Treaties and International Law in European History: From the Late Middle Ages to World War One. Cambridge: Cambridge University Press, 2004. ISBN 978-0-521-82724-9.

Lucas, Henry S., The Renaissance and the Reformation (New York: Harper and Brothers, 1960).

Mallett, Michael and Shaw, Christine, The Italian Wars: 1494–1559 (Harlow, England: Pearson Education, Inc., 2012). ISBN 978-0-582-05758-6.

Morris, T.A. Europe and England in the Sixteenth Century. London: Routledge, 2002. ISBN 0-203-01463-4.

Norwich, John Julius. A History of Venice. New York: Vintage Books, 1989. ISBN 0-679-72197-5.

Oman, Charles. A History of the Art of War in the Sixteenth Century. London: Methuen & Co., 1937.

Phillips, Charles and Alan Axelrod. Encyclopedia of Wars. 3 vols. New York: Facts on File, 2005. ISBN 0-8160-2851-6.

Taylor, Frederick Lewis. The Art of War in Italy, 1494–1529. Westport, Conn.: Greenwood Press, 1973. ISBN 0-8371-5025-6

Free Books by Charles River Editors

We have brand new titles available for free most days of the week. To see which of our titles are currently free, click on this link.

Discounted Books by Charles River Editors

We have titles at a discount price of just 99 cents everyday. To see which of our titles are currently 99 cents, click on this link.

Made in the USA
San Bernardino, CA
01 July 2020

74760826R00027